instant DRUMMING

D1604612

instant DRUMMING

PATRICK BYRNE

Quick and Easy Instruction
for the
Table-Top Drummer

Hal Leonard Publishing Corporation
7777 West Bluemound Road P.O. Box 13819 Milwaukee, WI 53213

O.K., so you're not a professional drummer, yet!

Well, neither am I. But, just like you, I love to drum along with my favorite music and that's why I wrote this book. If your dream is to one day play drums in a rock group, then *Instant Drumming* can help you get started.

Perhaps you don't want to play drums in a band but are still very interested in exploring the rock, Latin and swing rhythms that are used in most of today's popular music. If so, *Instant Drumming* gives you an entertaining introduction to two of the most essential elements of music the world over: beat and rhythm.

Maybe all you really want to do is learn a little bit more about the table-top drumming that you are already doing. Well, this book is written so that anyone who wants to play a mean beat on the kitchen table can have fun learning more about the percussive nature of music.

Patrick Byrne

Table of Contents

chapter 1

chapter 2

chapter 3

EXPLORING THE WORLD
OF DRUMMING

chapter 4

GETTING BETTER

chapter **1**

Getting Started

It's A Snap!

Are you the type of person who can't keep your hands or feet still when you listen to your favorite music? Do you just have to tap out the rhythm or somehow move to the beat? When you are driving your car with the radio playing, do you often find yourself drumming along on your steering wheel? If so, *Instant Drumming* will show you how to take your natural love of beat and rhythm one step further as you learn some of the basic techniques of drumming.

Just in case you thought that this might be hard work, here's a little rap that will give you a good idea of how easy and fun *Instant Drumming* will be. Just rap the lyrics and snap your fingers at each ✗:

finger snap	✗		✗		✗		✗	
	Hear	that	rhy - thm	and	feel	that	beat.	
	✗		✗		✗		✗	
	Clap	your	hands	and	tap	your	feet!	
	✗		✗		✗		✗	
	In - *stant*		*Drum - ming*	makes	it eas - y	as can	be	to
	✗		✗		✗		✗	
	play	a	drum		in - stant - ly!			

Beat It

What you just snapped your fingers to was, of course, the **beat.** Beat is such a basic element of music the world over that just about everybody has an instinctive feel for what it is. While it is true that some people can't carry a tune in a bucket, everyone can tap out a beat or clap a rhythm.

Your awareness of the beat began even before you were born. Think about it, your mother's beating heart was among the first sounds that your developing ears heard while you were still in the womb. As an infant you cooed to the soothing, swaying beat of the lullabies your parents sang to you. In school you enjoyed moving to music with different beats: the marches, dances, and songs of childhood. Your adolescence was probably accompanied by the driving beat of popular music.

Adult musical tastes usually broaden to include jazz, country, classical, folk, new age, or any of the many other styles that make up today's varied music scene. No matter how different these musical styles may sound on the surface, they are all held together by the very same thing. You guessed it, the beat.

Not Much To Look At

If we could draw a picture of the beat, it would look something like this, a simple series of evenly spaced lines:

| | | | | | | | | | | | | | | | | | |

Beats are evenly spaced pulses as represented by this series of evenly spaced lines.

Fast Or Slow, Keep It Steady

The musical beat is much like your own pulse. The speed or **tempo** of the beat can change depending on the type of music that is being played: it can be fast, slow, or anywhere in between. But, no matter what the tempo is, the beat is always a steady pulse:

The beat can be slow (widely spaced), fast (closely spaced), or anywhere in-between. No matter what the speed, the beats are always evenly spaced.

Counting Beats Not Sheep

Feeling the beat is an important first step toward becoming a drummer. You, like everyone else, took that first step when you were a child. To take the next step you need to understand what your body has naturally felt for years.

Musicians usually begin this process by counting the beat. But since most songs are hundreds of beats long, counting the beats straight through from the beginning to the end, as if they were sheep, will *never work*. This method of counting will probably put you to sleep, and it is certainly not the way anyone *feels* the beat.

How It Really Feels

You see, although drummers always play beats evenly they do not play them equally. In other words, some of the evenly spaced beats are **accented** or played louder than the others.

Compare this picture of the beat with the one on page ten, and you will see what a difference the accents make:

▌ | | | ▌ | | | ▌ | | |

Beats are always evenly spaced with some beats being accented or played louder than others.

Notice that the accents themselves are evenly spaced. This steady flow of accented and unaccented beats forms a series of units called **measures**. So, instead of counting beats from 1…to…say…300, drummers count beats the way that they feel them, in measures of 2 to 12 beats each:

1 2 3 4 **1** 2 3 4 **1** 2 3 4

Beats are counted in groups called measures. The first beat of each measure is accented.

This organization of beats into measures is called **meter**. Once a metric pattern like **1**234 is established it is usually repeated over and over for the course of the entire song.

"Brother Beat"

"Brother Beat" will help you better understand the concepts of beat and meter. Sing it to the tune of "Brother John" (*Frère Jacques*) and snap your fingers, clap your hands, or tap your foot at the ✗s:

✗	✗	✗	✗	✗	✗	✗	✗
1	2	3	4	**1**	2	3	4
Are	you	e	- ven,	are	you	e	- ven,

✗	✗	✗	✗	✗	✗	✗	✗
1	2	3	4	**1**	2	3	4
Broth	- er	Beat?		Broth	- er	Beat?	Be

✗	✗	✗	✗	✗	✗	✗	✗
1	2	3	4	**1**	2	3	4
Sure the	beats are	stead	- y. Be	sure the	beats	are e	- ven. Ac-

✗	✗	✗	✗	✗	✗	✗	✗
1	2	3	4	**1**	2	3	4
cent	beat	one.	Ac -	cent	beat	one.	

What Is A Drum?

Counting the beat is a cinch compared with trying to count all the different types of drums that are played throughout the world. The dictionary definition of the drum goes something like this:

> "…hollow cylinder…tightly stretched membrane…played with the hands or sticks…"

Yep, that's a drum all right, but why stop there? In *Instant Drumming* we use a much broader idea of what a drum is. For us, a drum is *anything* that you can drum on even if, according to the dictionary, it is not really a drum. The basic information about the beat and rhythm that you'll learn in *Instant Drumming* can be used with any "real" drum as well as table tops, chairs, wine glasses, your legs, a steering wheel…you name it!

Free Drums

Of course, in order to get the most you can out of *Instant Drumming* you need to have something to drum on but that doesn't mean that you should run out and spend some of your hard earned cash to buy a drum. No, everything in *Instant Drumming* can be played on just about anything that makes a sound when you tap on it.

Spend a little time as a sound scavenger and you will be amazed at how many FREE drums you can find lying around your house just waiting for you to elevate them from their humble daily existence to the exhalted level of drumhood. Table tops, books, buckets, pots and pans can all be used as drums. The only limits on what you can use are your imagination and the permission of whoever owns the "drum."

When the time comes for you to buy a drum, you will find some helpful consumer tips on pages 62-63.

Be Sure It Goes Thwump In The Night

To get started with *Instant Drumming* you will need at least one drum that goes "thwump." Two things determine a drum's sound: its size and what it is made of. For example, a thick book like *War and Peace* will have a much different sound than *Mad Magazine*; a solid oak table will not sound the same as a snack tray; and a steel bucket will have a much different thwump than a vinyl one. Experiment with what's available, and find a thwumper that will work for you.

Hands Now, Sticks Later

The easiest and most natural way for you to start drumming is to use your bare hands. In fact, many drums are meant to be played using your hands: bongos, congas, tablas, etc. In the "Table-Top Drumming" section that follows we will concentrate on getting your hands thwumping. Stick playing will be introduced when we get to the "Rock Drumming" section on page 24.

chapter
2

The Art of
Table-Top Drumming

You Have Two Hands

You can immediately improve your drumming by learning how to use your hands properly. When drummers play fast they alternate between their right and left hands for two important reasons: switching hands makes it easier to play the rhythms more accurately; and you can play much faster with two hands than you can using only one hand.

Play these two familiar rhythm patterns by saying the words and drumming the rhythms indicated by the ✗s. Use both hands (**L** = left and **R** = right) and don't forget to accent the "ones" as you tap the beat with your foot:

✗		✗		✗		✗		✗			✗
R		L		R		L		R			L
Yank	-	ee		doo	-	dle		Dan	-		dy
1				2				3			4

✗		✗	✗	✗		✗		✗		✗
R		L	R	L		R		L		R
Shave		and	a	hair	-	cut		two		bits!
1				2				3		4

Once you get the hang of drumming with both hands you'll really have some fun playing the next two songs: "Rummage Rap" and "Old MacDonald's Drums."

"Rummage Rap"

Line 1:
✗	✗	✗	✗	✗	✗	✗	✗	✗	✗
R	L	R	L	R	L	R	L	R	L
Search	the	kit -	chen	and	the	base	- ment	too.	Play
1	2	3	4			**1**	2	3	4

Line 2:
✗	✗	✗	✗	✗	✗	✗	✗	✗	✗
R	L	R	L	R	L	R	L	R	L
Pots,	pans	ta -	ble	tops	and	books	from	school.	You
1	2	3	4			**1**	2	3	4

Line 3:
✗	✗	✗	✗	✗	✗	✗	✗	✗	✗
R	L	R	L	R	L	R	L	R	L
can't	go	wrong,	use	your	ears,	it's	a	snap	to
1	2	3	4		**1**	2		3	4

Line 4:
✗	✗	✗	✗	✗	✗	✗	✗	✗	✗
R	L	R	L	R	L	R	L	R	L
find	the	best	sounds	for	the	rum	- mage	rap!	
1		2	3	4		**1**	2	3	4

"Old MacDonald's Drums"

X	X	X	X	X	X	X	X
R	L	R	L	R	L	R	L
Yes,	your	house	is	full	of	drums	
1	2	3	4	**1**	2	3	4

X	X	X	X	X	X	X	X
R	L	R	L	R	L	R	L
And	they're	all	for	free!			They
1	2	3	4	**1**	2	3	4

X	X	X	X	X	X	X	X	X
R	L	R	L	R	L	R	L	R
look	like	ta	- bles,	books	and	chairs	but	they
1	2	3	4	**1**	2	3	4	

X	X	X	X	X	X	X	X	X
L	R	L	R	L	R	L	R	L
look	like	drums	to	me.			With	a
1	2	3	4	**1**	2	3	4	

System 1

X	x	x	x	x	X	x	x	x
R	L	R	L	R	L	R	L	
thwump	thwump	here	and	a	thwump	thwump	there,	
1	2	3	4		**1**	2	3	4

System 2

X	x	x	x	x	x	X	x	x	x	x	x
R	L	R	L	R	L	R	L	R	L	R	L
Here	a	thwump,	there	a	thwump,	ev	-	'ry - where	a	thwump	thwump
1		2	3		4	**1**		2		3	4

System 3

X	x	x	x	X	x	x	x
R	L	R	L	R	L	R	L
In	your	house	there	are	some	drums	
1	2	3	4	**1**	2	3	4

System 4

X	x	x	x	X	x	x	x
R	L	R	L	R	L	R	L
And	they're	all	for	free!			
1	2	3	4	**1**	2	3	4

Rock Drumming

Layers Of Sound

The recordings that you listen to everyday are made up of **layers of sound**. The two stereo channels have been carefully mixed down from a multi-track master that might have had as many as 64 separate tracks.

Traditionally, during a live performance the multiple layers of sound were blended by a conductor or the musicians themselves as they played. By modern standards such an approach is hopelessly old-fashioned. Today, with the aid of digital electronics, most "live" performances are actually the result of a sound engineer combining live and pre-recorded layers of sound.

Well, no matter how sophisticated these techniques become, drummers are still the mix-master of the band as they play several layers of sound simultaneously:

The **primary layer** is the steady pulse of the beat that supports everything else:

1   2   3   4

On top of this steady pulse is added a layer of **metric accents**:

1   2   3   4

Finally, over this solid foundation is added at least one **rhythm pattern**:

✗   *✗*   *✗* *✗* *✗*

Your Drum Set

It will be easier for you to keep these layers of sound straight if you play each one on a different drum. That's why rock drummers use drum sets that consist of at least three or four drums and a number of cymbals. If you want to get a good rock groove going, the time has come for you to consider adding more sounds to your own drum set.

THWUMP — The thwump drum that you have been using so far will continue to be your main drum. For more variety add another thwump that is higher or lower in sound. Remember both the size and the material of an object determines the highness or lowness of its thwump.

PING — The next sound that you want to add to the basic thwump is a "ping." Drummers use metal cymbals to add a ping sound to their playing. You can get the same effect by using the lid from a pot or pan. Suspend the lid with a piece of string, and you will have a sound close to that of a cymbal. As with the thwump, it doesn't hurt to have several ping sounds to choose from.

TING — For advanced sound scavengers there is also a wide variety of sounds that can be made by *gently* tapping on a piece of glassware. Obviously, glass will break if it is hit too hard so use some care not to play the glass too roughly. With glassware you want a bell-like ting, not a heavy-metal thwump!

As an option, all of the rock material in *Instant Drumming* can still be played on a table top or a single drum. Just use the hands indicated in the examples, and be sure that you play the left-hand parts a little louder than those played by your right hand.

Sticks

Objects like a pot lid or a soda bottle will not ting or ping unless you play them with some sort of stick. You can either buy a pair of drum sticks (they only cost a few dollars) or simply use pencils, wooden spoons, etc. Pencils give you the added option of two different sounds depending on which end (the wooden one or the one with the eraser) you use.

Whatever type of sticks you choose, hold them using what drummers call **matched grip**. The "match" is that both hands hold the sticks in exactly the same way, between the thumb and forefinger as shown on the next page.

Don't let the term "grip" mislead you. Forget about tennis, baseball, and golf. Drum sticks should be held *just tightly enough to keep them from falling out of your hands*. Your grip should be loose because you want the stick to *bounce* up, away from the drum when you strike it. As you become a more advanced drummer, controlling stick bounce will be an important part of your drumming technique. Even as a beginning table-top tapper you will be much more comfortable, and play much better, if you always keep your grip as loose and relaxed as possible.

Foot Notes

Don't forget about your foot. The steady beat that you tap with your foot is an important part of the rock sound, and it needs to be heard. A linoleum or wood floor is your best bet, but a piece of cardboard or plywood will also work, even if the floor beneath it is carpeted.

The Rock Pattern

Approximately 99.99% of all rock songs, from "Rock Around The Clock" to the latest hit off of the radio, use the same basic rock pattern. This pattern consists of three layers of sound played by your foot and your two hands:

FOOT — Simply play the 4 meter over and over. This will create a solid foundation for the rhythm that will be played by your hands. In the example below, **bar lines** (|) are added to help you *see* where each measure begins and ends. The double-bar **repeat sign** (:‖) at the end of the pattern means that you should play the pattern over again without stopping. (Normally you will repeat the pattern until either the song or the section is over.) The "**&**" (and) added between the beats will help you play more accurately. Tap the beat (numbers) with your foot and count aloud : *1 and 2 and 3 and 4 and…*

Foot										
1	&	2	&	3	&	4	&	**1**	&	2	&	3	&	4	&

Always remember, in order for rock to sound like rock, this beat must be played …well…steady as a rock! Don't rush the beat or let it drag. To repeat, the feel of any rock pattern depends on this simple foundation being STEADY AS A ROCK.

RIGHT HAND (RH) — This pattern will sound best if it is played on something with a nice ping sound, like that of a cymbal:

RH	X		X		X		X		X		X		X		X		
Foot	▮		I		I		I		▮		I		I		I		
	1	&	2	&	3	&	4	&	**1**	&	2	&	3	&	4	&	

So far so good, but this pattern probably doesn't sound very much like rock to you. Well, the last layer of sound is the one that makes it rock.

LEFT HAND (LH) — This pattern adds a loud thwump on beats two and four of each measure creating a feeling of tension between these very strong rhythmic accents and the metric accent being played by your foot:

LH		**2**		**4**
Foot	**1**	2	3	4

It is this tension that instantly gives this pattern a rock feel:

BASIC ROCK PATTERN (complete)

RH	X		X		X		X		X		X		X		X		
LH			**X**				**X**				**X**				**X**		
Foot	▮		I		I		I		▮		I		I		I		
	1	&	2	&	3	&	4	&	**1**	&	2	&	3	&	4	&	

Double Play

Rock drummers very often play a simple variation of the basic rock beat by doubling the speed of the notes that they are playing with their right hand. These faster notes are called **eighth notes** and they are played at the rate of two taps per beat:

RH	X	X	X	X	X	X	X	X	X	X	X	X	X	X	X	X
	1	&	2	&	3	&	4	&	**1**	&	2	&	3	&	4	&

Now try the basic rock pattern with eighth notes:

RH	X	X	X	X	X	X	X	X	X	X	X	X	X	X	X	X
LH			X				X				X				X	
Foot	I		I		I		I		I		I		I		I	
	1	&	2	&	3	&	4	&	**1**	&	2	&	3	&	4	&

Rock Variations

Since the rock-beat pattern is used for at least part of almost every rock song ever written, drummers are constantly coming up with their own variations of the basic pattern. Here are some variations that you can try. See if you can create some of your own:

BASIC ROCK PATTERN (Variation 1)

	1	&	2	&	3	&	4	&	1	&	2	&	3	&	4	&
RH	X		X		X		X		X		X		X		X	
LH			X	X			X				X	X			X	
Foot	I		I		I		I		I		I		I		I	

BASIC ROCK PATTERN (Variation 2)

	1	&	2	&	3	&	4	&	1	&	2	&	3	&	4	&
RH	X		X		X		X		X		X		X		X	
LH			X			X	X	X			X			X	X	X
Foot	I		I		I		I		I		I		I		I	

BASIC ROCK PATTERN (Variation 3)

RH	✗	✗	✗	✗	✗	✗	✗	✗	✗	✗	✗	✗	✗	✗	✗	✗
LH			✗				✗	✗	✗			✗			✗	✗	✗
Foot	▮		│		│		│		▮		│		│		│	
	1	&	2	&	3	&	4	&	**1**	&	2	&	3	&	4	&

BASIC ROCK PATTERN (Variation 4)

RH	✗	✗	✗	✗	✗	✗	✗	✗	✗	✗	✗	✗	✗	✗	✗	✗
LH			✗				✗		✗		✗		✗		✗		
Foot	▮		│		│		│		▮		│		│		│	
	1	&	2	&	3	&	4	&	**1**	&	2	&	3	&	4	&

BASIC ROCK PATTERN (Variation 5)

RH	✗		✗		✗		✗		✗		✗		✗		✗	
LH			✗		✗	✗	✗				✗	✗			✗		
Foot	▮		│		│		│		▮		│		│		│	
	1	&	2	&	3	&	4	&	**1**	&	2	&	3	&	4	&

Four To A Beat

Rock drummers often play notes that are even faster than eighth notes. These notes are called **sixteenth notes** and they are played at the rate of four to a beat. In other words, they are played exactly *twice* as fast as eighth notes. When you first try playing sixteenth notes it is a good idea to use a very slow beat. As you get better you can use a faster tempo. For accuracy, music containing sixteenth notes should always be counted "one-ee-and-a-two-ee-and-a…":

BASIC ROCK PATTERN (Variation 6)

```
RH  X X X X X X X X X X X X X X X X | X X X X X X X X X X X X X X X X
LH        X             X           |         X   X           X
Foot |      |     |       |         | |       |     |       |
    1 ee & a 2 ee & a 3 ee & a 4 ee & a | 1 ee & a 2 ee & a 3 ee & a 4 ee & a
```

BASIC ROCK PATTERN (Variation 7)

```
RH  X X X X X X X X X X X X X X X X | X X X X X X X X X X X X X X X X
LH  x   x  X x       x       X    x | x   x  X x       x       X   X x
Foot |      |     |       |         | |       |     |       |
    1 ee & a 2 ee & a 3 ee & a 4 ee & a | 1 ee & a 2 ee & a 3 ee & a 4 ee & a
```

Fancy Footwork

If you haven't done so already, be sure that your right foot is tapping on a hard surface. Your right foot's most important role in the rock sound is to keep the beat steady. Drummers can play some very interesting rhythms with their foot without disrupting the flow of the beat. On a real drum set the right foot plays on a pedal that is attached to a padded striker. Each time the drummer's foot taps the pedal the striker pounds the bass drum producing a loud thud. In order to get the right feel for these next three patterns your right foot needs to be just as loud as the sound of the other drums that you are playing.

BASIC ROCK PATTERN *(Variation 8)*

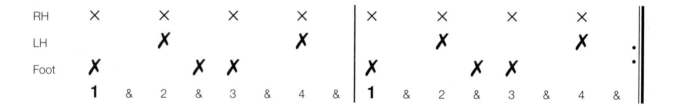

You may want to practice each hand alone with the foot since playing three layers of sound can be a little tricky on the first try. Practice each layer alone, then two layers together, and finally all three layers at the same time.

BASIC ROCK PATTERN *(Variation 9)*

	1	&	2	&	3	&	4	&	1	&	2	&	3	&	4	&
RH	✗		✗		✗		✗		✗		✗		✗		✗	
LH			✗				✗				✗				✗	
Foot	✗				✗	✗			✗				✗	✗	✗		✗

BASIC ROCK PATTERN *(Variation 10)*

	1	&	2	&	3	&	4	&	1	&	2	&	3	&	4	&
RH	✗	✗	✗	✗	✗	✗	✗	✗	✗	✗	✗	✗	✗	✗	✗	✗
LH			✗				✗				✗				✗	
Foot	✗						✗		✗	✗				✗	✗		

Forming A Song

Playing the same pattern for an entire song would definitely be monotonous and sound boring. That is why drummers usually play a different pattern or variation for each part or **section** of a song. For example, a drummer might use 3 different variations of the basic pattern to play a typical, three-section rock song. We can call these variations: **A**, **B**, and **C**.

The plan or layout of the song might go something like this:

Section	Pattern/Variation
INTRODUCTION	A
1ST VERSE	B
CHORUS/REFRAIN	C
2ND VERSE	B
CHORUS/REFRAIN	C
BRIDGE	A
INSTRUMENTAL VERSE/GUITAR SOLO	B
CHORUS/REFRAIN	C
3RD VERSE	B
CHORUS/REFRAIN	C
CODA	C
OUTRO	A

Notice how each pattern/variation is used with a specific section of the song. For example, the verses are always **B**. In this way what the drummer plays matches the overall **form** of the song:

A B C B C A B C C A

Filling In The Blanks

Drummers play **fills** whenever they get a chance. Fills are mini-solos that are only one or two measures long. Drummers love fills for two reasons: they give them a chance to get away from the pattern for a few seconds; and they give them a chance to show off a little.

Here's a one measure fill that can be used *in place of* the last measure of the basic rock pattern. This fill would also work with just about any variation of this basic rock pattern. Notice that, during the fill, your foot stops playing (but don't stop counting!) while both hands play on two different thwump drums:

BASIC ROCK PATTERN with FILL 1

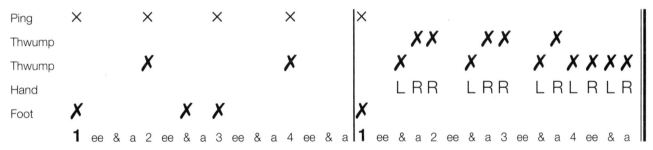

Immediately after playing a fill you should return to the pattern. Fills are most often used during the transition from one pattern to another, for example between a verse and a chorus. Fills can also be used whenever there is a melodic pause, for example when the singer or soloists takes a break between the phrases of the melody.

Fill 'Em Up

Here are a few more fills that can be used with most rock-pattern variations. As you gain experience, feel free to be creative and come up with your own ideas for fills. Remember that fills are used *in place of* a measure or two of the original pattern and that a fill should never disrupt the underlying beat.

FILL 2

	1	ee	&	a	2	ee	&	a	3	ee	&	a	4	ee	&	a
Ping	X															
Thwump			X	X			X	X								
Thwump	X				X				X	X	X	X	X	X	X	X
Hand	L		R	R	L		R	R	L	R	L	R	L	R	L	R
Foot	X															

FILL 3

	1	ee	&	a	2	ee	&	a	3	ee	&	a	4	ee	&	a
Ping	X															
Thwump			X				X			X		X		X		
Thwump	X				X				X		X		X		X	
Hand	L		R		L		R		L	R	L	R	L	R	L	
Foot	X															

Slow Rockin'

Rock ballads are usually love songs so they naturally tend to use a slower, more romantic beat than the basic rock pattern. Instead, you need to play a special slow-rock pattern. The heart of this slow-rock pattern is the **triplet**. As its name implies, triplets are played at the rate of *three notes to a beat*. Well-known songs that use this slow-rock pattern include Whitney Houston's "Saving All My Love For You," Journey's "Open Arms," and classic rock songs like "My Special Angel" and "Silhouettes."

The small "3" above the **✗**s in the examples given below show you where the triplets are. When playing triplets count 1-and-ah 2-and-ah 3-and-ah 4-and-ah as your foot taps each beat (number). Play this pattern slowly—remember this is *slow* rock—and give a slight accent to the first note of each set of triplets. Drummers usually play triplets on a cymbal with their strong hand (the right hand, for most people). Repeat this pattern several times until you feel comfortable with it and it seems to flow along effortlessly:

Triplets Two

The next step in playing the slow rock pattern is to add your left hand to the triplet pattern that you just learned. Drummers usually play this left-hand part on a snare drum. You can use your high thwump to get the same effect. Remember your right-hand part should still go ping:

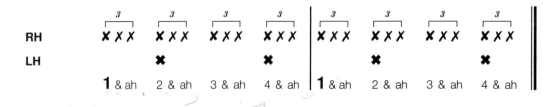

As with the basic rock pattern, drummers constantly come up with their own variations of this slow-rock pattern. Have fun creating some variations of your own. Remember, no matter how slow the rock is, the beat must always be steady!

Basic Latin Rhythms

The countries of South America, Mexico, and the Caribbean are home to some of the world's most exciting drum music. With musical roots reaching back to Africa, Latin music often features bongos and conga drums and is perfect for table-top tappers.

To get the right sound for all of these Latin rhythms use a high (RH) and a low (LH) drum:

CHA CHA

	1	&	2	&	3	&	4	&	1	&	2	&	3	&	4	&
RH	X		X		X		X		X		X		X	X	X	
LH			X				X	X	X		X				X	X :

CHA CHA (Variation 1)

	1	&	2	&	3	&	4	&	1	&	2	&	3	&	4	&
RH	X	X	X	X	X	X	X	X	X	X	X	X	X	X	X	X
LH			X				X	X			X				X	X :

CHA CHA (Variation 2)

	1	&	2	&	3	&	4	&	1	&	2	&	3	&	4	&
RH	X	X	X	X	X	X	X	X	X	X	X	X	X	X	X	X
LH			X				X	X			X			X	X	X :

Clave

The **clave** (pronounced CLAH-vay) pattern is the foundation of most Latin rhythms. It is named after the percussion instrument that it is usually played on, the *claves*: two thick sticks that look a little like wooden hot dogs. The two-measure clave pattern can start with *either* measure:

or, vice versa…

Clave Play

Here's one way of playing the clave pattern using eighth notes and both hands. Notice that the accents remain the same as the first example given on the previous page:

X	x	x	X	x	x	X	x	x	x	X	x	X	x	x	x
R	L	R	L	R	L	R	L	R	L	R	L	R	L	R	L
1	&	2	&	3	&	4	&	1	&	2	&	3	&	4	&

In the next example the only difference is that you start the clave pattern with your left hand instead of your right. Switching hands like this is a good way to be sure that both hands can really work together:

X	x	x	X	x	x	X	x	x	x	X	X	X	x	x	x
L	R	L	R	L	R	L	R	L	R	L	R	L	R	L	R
1	&	2	&	3	&	4	&	1	&	2	&	3	&	4	&

In this last clave example play the tricky second measure very carefully:

X	x	x	X	x	x	X	x	x		X		X	x	x	x
R	L	R	L	R	L	R	L	R		L		R	L	R	L
1	&	2	&	3	&	4	&	1	&	2	&	3	&	4	&

Some Classic Latin Rhythms

Over the years many Latin rhythms have found their way into the mainstream of popular music. Here are a few of these classic rhythms:

BEGUINE

Originally from the island of Martinique, this dance rhythm became the rage during the 1930s. Cole Porter, one of the great songwriters of that era, immortalized this rhythm with his song "Begin The Beguine:"

x	**X**		x	x	**X**	x	**X**	x	**X**		x	x	**X**	x	**X**
R	**L**		L	R	**L**	R	**R**	R	**L**		L	R	**L**	R	**R**
1	&	2	&	3	&	4	&	**1**	&	2	&	3	&	4	&

RHUMBA

The Rhumba (or rumba) comes from Cuba and was very popular in the 1940s and 1950s:

x	x	x	x	**X**	x	x	x	x	x	x	x	**X**	x	**X**	x
R	L	R	L	**R**	L	R	L	R	L	R	L	**R**	L	**R**	L
1	&	2	&	3	&	4	&	**1**	&	2	&	3	&	4	&

MAMBO

The mambo originated in Haiti and became one of the biggest dance fads of the 1950s:

	1	&	2	&	3	&	4	&	1	&	2	&	3	&	4	&
RH	X		X		X			X		X		X	X			
LH			X				X				X				X	X

SAMBA

The tempo of this dance rhythm from Brazil is usually in the range of medium slow to fast. The clave pattern is not used with the *samba*. Notice that the third beat of each measure is accented:

	1	&	2	&	3	&	4	&	1	&	2	&	3	&	4	&
X	X	X	X	X	**X**	X	X	X		X		X	**X**	X	X	
sticking	L	R	L	R	L	R	L	R		R		L	R	L	R	

BOSSA NOVA

Another Brazilian rhythm, the *bossa nova* uses the clave pattern except that the last note of the pattern is delayed, coming on the "and" of three instead of on the beat. The foot adds some interest to the sound by playing its own rhythm pattern. The *bossa nova* was very popular during the 1960s with "The Girl From Ipanema" being the best example of this style:

	1	&	2	&	3	&	4	&	1	&	2	&	3	&	4	&
RH	X	X	X	X	X	X	X	X	X	X	X	X	X	X	X	
LH	X			X			X				X			X		
Foot	X			X	X			X	X				X	X		X

48

Swing

Swing Time

Swing rhythm has been around for many years. The roots of jazz, blues, and dixieland all go back to the early days of this century. This basic rhythm is still with us today, in one form or another, in the music of most of your favorite musicians.

The easiest way to get into swing is to return to the triplet pattern that you learned in the section on slow rock:

RH
3	3	3	3		3	3	3	3
X X X	X X X	X X X	X X X	X X X	X X X	X X X	X X X
1 & ah	2 & ah	3 & ah	4 & ah	**1** & ah	2 & ah	3 & ah	4 & ah

In order to make this rhythm swing all you need to do is *skip* the middle triplet (✗   ✗) so that you play the first and third notes of each triplet. Give a little bit of an accent to the first note of each set:

RH
3	3	3	3		3	3	3	3
X X	X X	X X	X X	X X	X X	X X	X X
1 & ah	2 & ah	3 & ah	4 & ah	**1** & ah	2 & ah	3 & ah	4 & ah

Shuffle Along

When you play the next example correctly it should have an uneven feel that no longer sounds like slow-rock. That's because it isn't. What you are now playing is called a shuffle, a term that describes exactly how this pattern sounds and feels:

RH

| 3 | 3 | 3 | 3 | 3 | 3 | 3 | 3 |

x x x x x x x x | x x x x x x x x :||

1 & ah   2 & ah   3 & ah   4 & ah | 1 & ah   2 & ah   3 & ah   4 & ah

Practice this shuffle pattern at different tempos. When you can comfortably play it at a medium tempo try adding the left hand as shown here:

RH

| 3 | 3 | 3 | 3 | 3 | 3 | 3 | 3 |

x x x x x x x x | x x x x x x x x

LH

x x | x x

1 & ah   2 & ah   3 & ah   4 & ah | 1 & ah   2 & ah   3 & ah   4 & ah

By now you can safely drop the "and ah" from your counting. If the steadiness of the beat begins to waver or the skipping feeling of your hands becomes too even, put the "and ah" back in, and practice the above patterns some more before going on.

RH

| 3 | 3 | 3 | 3 | 3 | 3 | 3 | 3 |

x x x x x x x x | x x x x x x x x

LH

x x | x x

1   2   3   4 | 1   2   3   4

The Real Swing

With each of these examples you have been getting closer and closer to the authentic swing rhythm from which both the shuffle and slow-rock rhythms originally evolved during the early days of rock and roll. The real swing rhythm pattern goes like this:

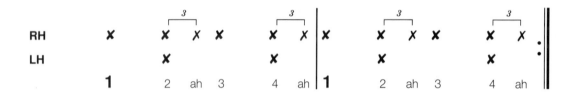

During the pre-rock era this rhythm was the backbone of the big band sound of the 1930s and 1940s. Today it is still heard in rhythm and blues and other popular styles with roots in this era.

chapter 3

Exploring the World of Drumming

Older Than Old

Drumming has been around for many thousands of years. In fact, it is very possible that the drum was the first musical instrument ever invented.

Our prehistoric ancestors used various objects like sticks, rocks, and bones along with hand clapping, foot stomping, and body slapping to accompany their dancing, chanting and singing. One day a cave person tapped on a hollow object such as an inverted bowl, a hollowed-out log, or, perhaps, even a skull and the thwump was born! The basic design of the drum has changed very little since that first thwump.

Back To Basics

Post-industrial society seems far removed from the ancient magic of drumming. New musical technology is everywhere. Sometimes it appears that the cutting edge is where everyone wants to be. Yet, the low-tech drum offers something that all of the latest high-tech electronic gizmos just can't: the personal satisfaction that comes from using either your bare hands or wooden sticks to play an instrument that was carefully crafted from wood, animal skin, and metal.

World Music

World Music is the term currently used to describe any music that comes from outside of the traditions of European and American popular and classical music. As is the case with terms like *New Age* and *Folk Music*, World Music defies a simple, all-encompassing definition. In the "World Music" bin at your local music store you can find music as diverse as: Bulgarian a cappella choruses; Indian ragas; Buddhist ceremonial music; Eskimo tribal chants; and Irish jigs and reels. The common philosophical thread that unites this hodgepodge is a world view that sees in this diversity the essential unity of human experience.

This is really nothing new. "Ethnic" or "International" music has often been a very important part of our culture. During the 1940s and 1950s Latin music became a permanent part of popular music through the lively performances of, among others, Xavier Cugat, Carmen Miranda and Desi Arnez. In the 1960s, Ravi Shankar, with the help of the Beatles, brought Indian music to a larger audience. In the 1970s Jamaican reggae began achieving lasting popularity through the music of Jimmy Cliff and Bob Marley. And in the 1980s Paul Simon's hit album *Graceland* featured many South African musicians.

For drummers, each of these trends has brought with it a whole new group of rhythms to learn and master as well as a new approach to the role of drumming and percussion in the music. This is likely to be the case no matter what the next non-western musical import is.

The World View

It is impossible to explain in a few words the many differences that exist between our European/American approach to music and that used in other cultures. Probably the most significant difference is that westerners seem to get bound up in thinking about instruments, technique, and notation. Rather than focusing on the *spirit* of the music, these *things* tend to become the object of our music making. In other cultures the traditional musicians view their music as a reflection of their physical and spiritual environment. To them music is a mixture of sound, magic, and ritual.

Mother Drum

World Music offers drummers a vast new area of rhythms to be explored. Mickey Hart, the long-time drummer for the rock group the Grateful Dead, has produced two wonderful albums of percussion music that will give you a good idea of what this kind of drum music is like: *At The Edge* and *Planet Drum* (both on the Ryko label). *Planet Drum* won a 1992 Grammy as "Record Of The Year" in the World Music category and a similar award in a readers poll conducted by *Down Beat* magazine. Hart's approach to this music is detailed in his book *Planet Drum: A Celebration of Percussion and Rhythm* (HarperSanFrancisco, publisher). If you are seriously interested in exploring the wide world of drumming or just curious, Hart's tapes and book are an excellent place to start.

chapter

4

Getting Better

Holistic Practice...Your Next Steps

Whenever you practice your main goal should be to focus on the music that you are playing. Sometimes you will get stuck because you are thinking too hard about how to play a rhythm pattern rather than how it should feel. On the other hand sometimes you will get stuck when you try to play a pattern too fast simply because that is "how it should go." These are both common mistakes that all musicians have to overcome.

Just remember that no matter how fast a pattern *should* be played, you always want to start off by practicing it at a *very slow* tempo. Slow-motion practice allows your mind the time it needs to figure a pattern out . Once your mind figures out how to play a pattern, your body will gradually begin to take over as you pick up the tempo and get a feel for how it should be played. As you progress as a drummer your mind and body will begin working together as one and this oneness is the ultimate goal of any musical training.

With time, the slow-motion process will gradually take much less time because you will begin to sense how a pattern should be played the first time you hear it played or see it printed in a book. When this starts happening you know you have become a real drummer!

Drumming With Your Ears

Your interest in drumming undoubtedly began the first time that you heard a drummer, either live or on a recording, play in such a way that you were inspired to drum along with the music. As you continue to learn more about drumming you need to keep renewing that inspiration, and the best way to do that is to listen to other drummers whenever and wherever you can. Listen to your favorite music, but also stretch out once in a while by listening to different kinds of music than you normally don't listen to.

You will learn a lot of new things just by listening to master drummers, like new patterns and flashy fills. But more important than their playing you'll get a *feeling* for what drumming is all about. It's real easy to find books that contain thousands of patterns and fills. But, unless you already have a *feel* for the music, this material will be worthless to you.

There's only one way that you can get and keep this *feel*: listen, listen, and then listen some more!.

Buying Your First Drum

- **Listen to the music** — Listen to recordings or live performances of the style of music that you want to play. Find out what kind of drums are being used to play this music.
- **Talk with drummers** — Talk to drummers who play the style of music that you want to play. If they seem knowledgeable, ask them for advice about choosing a drum. They will usually be glad to help.
- **Do some research** — Drummers are gearheads so drum magazines are loaded with flashy ads for the latest must-haves. Read the articles and interviews sandwiched between the ads, and you'll get a pretty good idea of what the drum market is like.
- **Shop around** — Each music store is a unique experience so shop around. In larger urban areas you might even find a shop that sells nothing but drums. If you can get to one of these it would definitely be worth a trip just to see and play the wide variety of drums that are currently available.
- **Make a contact** — Try to find an up-to-date salesperson who can answer all of your questions without making you feel like a moron. Remember, a salesperson's livelihood depends on making *sales*. Try to get information without wasting their time, especially when you are "just browsing" and really have no intention of making an immediate purchase. When you do find a good salesperson, ask for their business card and then be sure to ask for them by name when you return to that store to buy your drum.

- **Try it out** — *Never* buy a drum that you haven't played. The store should have a room set aside where you can do this in private for a reasonable amount of time. Remember, there are just as many variables in buying a drum as there are in buying a pair of shoes, so be sure the drum that you buy fits.

QUICK & EASY INSTRUCTION FOR ABS BEGINNE

INSTANT DRUMMING

If you're a table-top drum... Here is a fun guide to the world of beat, rhythm, and personal percussion. *Instant Drumming* takes the mystery out of African and Latin rhythms and will have you drumming them on table tops, pots and pans, or *any* drum in no time. The text and many humorous illustrations make *Instant Drumming* an excellent way for you to get down to the heart of music. *Instant Drumming* is the music book that **can** be beat!
00330047..$6.95

INSTANT HARMONICA

Instant Harmonica is the book that makes learning harmonica fun and easy. In no time at all, students will be blowing a variety of tunes on their harp. The book includes a combination of t... lature and EZ-Play® notation and over thirty all-t... great country and folk songs. Works with any ten-h... harmonica.
00330046..$6...

INSTANT KEYBOARD

Quick & Easy Instruction For The Impatient Student!

With the aid of this book, even the individual who doesn't know a quarter note from a bank n... can have fun with the portable keyboard. The easy-to-follow four-part instruction takes you fr... the absolute music basics right up through some musical "tricks of the trade" to dress up y... playing style. A comprehensive chord chart is also provided for those who choose to play fingered chords.
00183575..$9...

PLAY GUITAR WITHOUT FRETTING

"Play Guitar Without Fretting" is the fun, easy and non-intimidating approach to learning to play the guitar, either on your own or with a teacher. Using a unique "Quick Start"... progresses more ...ing. More than 90 songs surroun... ...ideal beginning method for those ... ...e frustrated "guitar lesson dropou... ....$9...

...UT FRETTING

...more than 500 ...rds in a well- ...Each chord is ...ent fingerings, ...makes locating chords easier ...Guitar Without Fretting." ....$5...

...music dealer, or write to:

...g Corporation

Prices, contents and availability subject to change without notice.